Start Smart Guide to Brand Differentiation

Juliana A. Taylor

ISBN: 1494856050
ISBN-13: 978-1494856052

DEDICATION

As with our first book the *Start Smart Business Plan Guide*, this book is dedicated to the very people that it was written to help - entrepreneurs. As you embark on this rewarding journey, I hope that the tools that this book provides will make the path clearer and easier to navigate.

Dear Reader,

It's a pleasure to share our third publication, the *Start Smart Guide to Brand Differentiation*. As entrepreneurs we have experienced the challenges that are associated with creating a strong and distinct brand identity, and this book explores the process from both a theoretical and practical perspective.

As with our other resources, by purchasing our book, you have already begun to apply two of the most important concepts in the world of entrepreneurship:

Learning. As an entrepreneur it is essential to continuously learn and build knowledge on your industry, customers, competition and product(s).

Planning. Do not let the world take you by surprise. Small business owners in particular tend to be more heavily impacted by changes in their business environment. This is because their market is often narrower and their resources more limited. It is therefore important to do your best to plan ahead, so that when the unexpected does arise, you will be able to do something about it.

To learn more about us and how we can help your business, visit www.startsmartgh.com.

Happy reading!

Best Wishes
Juliana A. Taylor & the Start Smart Team

CONTENTS

1 WHERE THIS BOOK FITS IN THE START SMART SERIES

The *Start Smart Guide to Brand Differentiation* is the third book in the Start Smart series. It marks a key milestone in our journey towards becoming a trusted source of knowledge and support for entrepreneurs in Ghana, and eventually across the African continent. Through our books, entrepreneurs are empowered with the tools necessary to:

- **Build a strong foundation** through the concepts discussed in the *Start Smart Business Plan Guide*

- **Showcase their business offerings** through the strategies developed in the *Start Smart Launch Roadmap*

- **Stay ahead of the competition** through the principles highlighted in this book, the *Start Smart Guide to Brand Differentiation*

As a supplement to our publications, Start Smart offers corresponding training courses. To learn more about our training offerings or how you can purchase the books in our series, please send an email to julianat@startsmartgh.com. Our books are also available for purchase online at amazon.com.

2 WHAT'S WRONG WITH BLENDING IN?

Successful businesses share a number of common traits including a clearly defined mission and vision, appropriately structured teams and processes for planning and execution, and a strong relationship with their customers. Another defining trait of successful brands is their ability to distinguish themselves from the competition. They are able to clearly and consistently communicate to customers what makes them different and why these differences matter. The marketing term for this concept is the Unique Selling Proposition (USP).

The term USP[1] was coined by Rosser Reeves to advocate an approach to advertising that focused on creating a compelling reason for customers to purchase products and services. Reeves' three requirements for a strong USP were:

- A clear linkage between purchasing the product/service and enjoying a particular set of benefits
- A well-differentiated proposition that competitors cannot or will not offer
- Existing demand for the product/service

Below are examples of brands that have succeeded in defining their USP.

Brand	Unique Selling Proposition (USP)
M&M's	"It melts in your mouth, not in your hands."
FedEx	"When it absolutely, positively has to be there overnight."
Domino's Pizza	"Hot, fresh pizza delivered in 30 minutes or less, guaranteed."
Toms Shoes	"One for One"
Kiva	"Empower people around the world with a $25 loan."

Figure 1 - Examples of Brand USPs

---

[1] Reeves, Rosser "Reality in Advertising"(1961)

From your experiences as a consumer, which brands have captured your attention and why? In the table below list examples of brands that you've purchased that you believe have a strong USP.

	Brand	Unique Selling Proposition (USP)
1		
2		
3		
4		

Figure 2 - Your Examples of Strong USPs

3 DO YOUR HOMEWORK

Self-Assessment

Brands, like people, can have a number of aspects to their "personalities". While this can make a brand more dynamic and potentially enable it to appeal to a broader audience; its personality must also make sense to consumers. Thus, when developing a USP, it is helpful for businesses to identify one "peg"/"personality trait" on which they can build their business identity, and eventually their marketing strategy. These "pegs" are also known as the 4 P's of marketing:

- Product characteristics:
- Price structure
- Placement strategy (location and distribution)
- Promotional strategy

The diagram below provides further detail on the 4 P's and how they relate to one another.

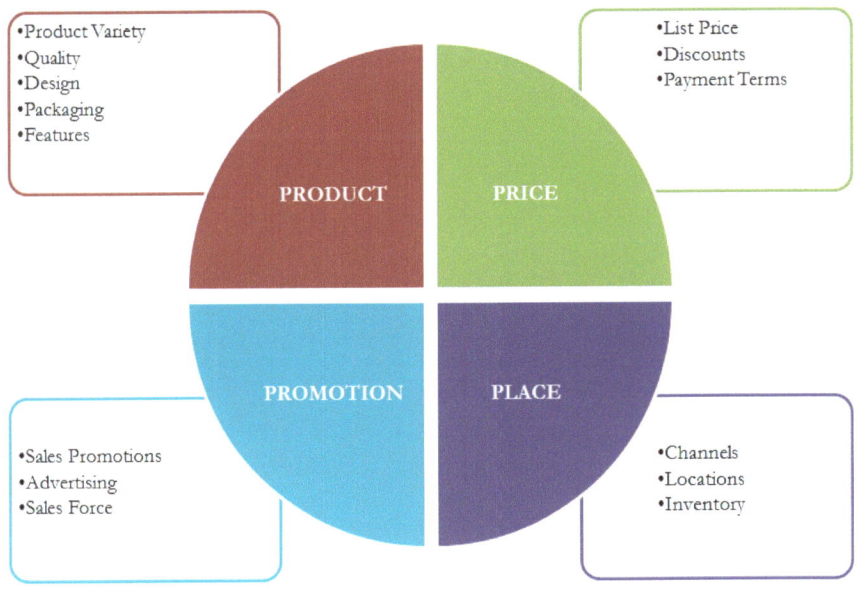

Figure 3 - 4 P's of Marketing

A classic example of a business identifying and making use of a "peg" is Hanes L'Eggs hosiery products. In an era in which hosiery was primarily sold in department stores, Hanes opened a new distribution channel for hosiery sales. The idea: Since hosiery was a consumer staple, why not sell it where other staples were sold--in grocery stores? That placement strategy then drove the company's selection of product packaging (a plastic egg) so the pantyhose did not seem incongruent in the supermarket.

Are there brands in your market that have adopted a similar strategy? Share them below.

....

....

....

....

....

....

....

....

....

....

....

....

In order to effectively use "pegs" to understand your business and define your USP, it is important to gain an understanding of:

- **Your Customer's Needs, Not Yours** - Too often, entrepreneurs fall in love with their product or service and forget that it is the customer's needs, not their own, that they must satisfy. It is important to step back from your daily operations and carefully scrutinize what your customers really want. If for example you own a pizzeria, customers may primarily patronize your location to find food. What will make them loyal repeat customers though? The answer may be as simple as a high quality product, convenience, reliability, friendliness, cleanliness and great service.

- **What Motivates Your Customers** – In some respects, effectively marketing your product/service to your customer requires you to be an "amateur psychologist". This is because you need to investigate what motivates your customer's decision making. You will therefore need to go beyond traditional measures such as age, gender, race, income level, geographic location and the differentiators we mentioned in the pizza example above to understand how customers think. Referencing the pizza example above again, understanding customer psychology includes knowing what people associate different pizza types with (i.e. luxury vs. cheap), understanding the impact of peer pressure etc.

In the space below assess:

1. Your perception of customer needs vs. actual needs

....

....

....

....

....

....

....

....

....

....

....

2. Factors that incentivize/motivate your target customers.

....

....

....

....

....

....

....

....

....

....

3. Traits that distinguish you from the competition

....

....

....

....

....

....

....

....

....

....

4. Factors that will maximize customer loyalty

....

....

....

....

....

....

....

....

5. Your USP

....

....

....

....

....

....

....

....

....

For additional guidance on how best to approach gathering this information reference the *Start Smart Business Plan Guide*.

External Research

While self-assessment is critical, it is also important to understand external data and the implications it could have for your business. Useful external sources include:

- **Industry Research** - Before you can discover what makes your product unique, you'll need to know what else is available for your prospective customers. That means doing in-depth analysis of each one of your competitors.
  - o What products/services exist that can fill the same needs as yours?
  - o What is their USP and which selling points do these competitors promote?

To answer these questions, it may be useful to review their external communications and marketing materials (e.g., websites, social media pages, newsletters, etc.). Reviews from independent review organizations and regulatory agencies can also provide useful insights.

....

....

....

....

....

....

....

....

....

....

- **Customer Feedback** - What do people who already own a competitor product or have used their services have to say? Customer reviews can be a goldmine of feedback, and can provide you with a great way to understand how you can differentiate yourself. These reviews provide a complete perspective including customer service experience, convenience, reliability, ease of use etc.

....

....

....

....

....

....

....

....

....

....

4. CREATE YOUR OWN

Take a moment to reflect on the insights and information that you've compiled thought the course of this book and assesses how close you are to defining your own USP. In the space below define your USP and determine how closely they align with Rosser Reeves' requirements that were described in Chapter 2. All the best!

Your USP
a.   Clearly defined linkage(s) between purchasing the product/service and a enjoying a particular set of benefits
b.   Well-differentiated proposition that competitors cannot or will not offer
c.   Existing Demand for the product/service

Start Smart

Notes

Notes

Notes

Notes

About the Author

Start Smart was founded by Juliana A. Taylor in 2011 to empower African entrepreneurs, through the provision of business and financial literacy tools. She has a strong interest in entrepreneurship and looks forward to contributing towards the development of African businesses.

Juliana holds a BA in Economics from Princeton University and a Masters in Management Studies from Duke University's Fuqua School of Business. She has also spent time working for Google in Ghana on its business and university outreach initiatives, and Accenture in Washington, D.C. as a consultant for federal, private sector and nonprofit clients.

Start Smart

www.ingramcontent.com/pod-product-compliance
Lightning Source LLC
Chambersburg PA
CBHW041622180526

45159CB00002BC/976